THROUGH THE PRISM OF LIFE: A COLLECTION OF POEMS

ALLEN JOY

Made with ♥ on the Notion Press Platform
www.notionpress.com

This book is dedicated to my loving family and my best friends Nimmy Treesa, Justin Paul, Alwin paul and Prankit Sahu, who have supported and encouraged me throughout my life. Your unwavering belief in my abilities has given me the strength to pursue my dreams and never give up. I am grateful for your constant love and support.

I also want to dedicate this book to my dear friends, who have been a source of inspiration and motivation for me. Your unwavering support, encouragement, and feedback have been invaluable, and I could not have done this without you.

Finally, I want to dedicate this book to all the readers out there. I hope this book brings you joy, inspiration, and a new perspective on life. Thank you for taking the time to read my work and supporting me on this journey.

Contents

Contents

Contents

Foreword

It is my pleasure to write the foreword for this book, "Through the Prism of Life" by Allen Joy. As a renowned poet and writer, Allen has captured the essence of life and the human experience through their eloquent and insightful poetry.

This anthology poem collection is a powerful reflection of the beauty and complexities of life, and Allen has a unique gift for illuminating the subtleties and nuances of the human experience. Their words are poignant, evocative, and deeply moving, offering readers a glimpse into the human heart and soul.

I have no doubt that this book will be a source of inspiration and comfort for readers, as it touches on the universal themes of love, loss, hope, and redemption. It is a testament to Author's talent and dedication to their craft, and I am honored to have been given the opportunity to read and share their work.

I highly recommend "Through the Prism of Life" to anyone who appreciates the art of poetry and the beauty of the written word. It is a true masterpiece and a valuable addition to readers.

Preface

I am delighted to present "Through the Prism of Life," an anthology poem collection that reflects my journey as a poet and writer. This book is a culmination of many years of hard work, dedication, and a deep passion for the art of poetry.

As a writer, I have always been fascinated by the complexities and nuances of life. Through my poetry, I have attempted to capture the beauty and fragility of the human experience and to offer a glimpse into the hearts and minds of people from all walks of life.

The poems in this book are inspired by my own experiences, observations, and interactions with the world around me. They are a reflection of my own struggles, joys, and hopes, and I hope that they resonate with readers in their own unique ways.

I am deeply grateful to all those who have supported and encouraged me along the way, including my family, friends, and fellow writers. I also want to express my heartfelt thanks to the readers, whose feedback and encouragement have been invaluable.

I hope that this book inspires readers to see the world through a different lens, to embrace the complexities of life, and to find beauty in even the most challenging moments. It is with great pleasure that I present "Through the Prism of Life" to the world.

Acknowledgements

Writing a book is not an easy feat, and it takes a lot of effort, time, and dedication to see it through. I am grateful to have had the opportunity to write this book and share my thoughts and experiences with readers.

First and foremost, I would like to express my sincere gratitude to the people who have supported me throughout this journey. To my family, who has always been my source of inspiration and strength, thank you for believing in me and encouraging me to pursue my passion. To my friends, who have been my sounding board and offered their honest feedback, thank you for your unwavering support.

I would also like to extend my thanks to the individuals who have helped me shape my ideas and refine my writing. To my editor, whose expertise and guidance have been invaluable, thank you for your patience and dedication. To my beta readers, who have provided me with constructive criticism and suggestions, thank you for your time and effort.

Lastly, I want to thank my readers for taking the time to read my book. Your interest and support mean the world to me, and I hope that this book has inspired you in some way.

Thank you all for being a part of this journey and for helping me bring "Through the Prism of Life" to life.

Prologue

Life is a journey, and every experience we encounter is like a prism, reflecting different facets of our existence. Some reflections are bright and beautiful, while others are dark and challenging. But all of them contribute to shaping our understanding of the world and ourselves.

In this book, I invite you to join me on a journey through the prism of life. Together, we will explore the many aspects of our human experience, from the joys and sorrows of love to the complexities of identity and purpose. Through personal anecdotes, philosophical musings, and reflections on cultural and historical events, we will delve deep into what it means to be alive.

I believe that every person's perspective on life is unique and valuable. As such, I hope this book will serve as a catalyst for your own reflections and musings. Whether you are seeking guidance, inspiration, or simply a new way of looking at things, my hope is that you will find something in these pages that resonates with you.

So come, let us journey together through the prism of life. Let us explore the many colors and hues that make up our human experience, and let us discover the beauty and meaning in even the most challenging of reflections.

Life and Love

1. Birth

From the darkness of the womb
Comes a new life, a fresh bloom
Tiny fingers and tiny toes
A brand new chapter, a story unfolds
With a cry, the newborn awakens
To a world full of wonder and amazement
The first breath, the first sound
A miracle of nature, a new life found
The parents rejoice, overwhelmed with love
A gift from above, a blessing from the heavens above
A new journey, a new adventure
A new beginning, a brand new venture
From this day on, the world will never be the same
A new voice, a new face, a new name
A little life with endless potential
The future is bright, the possibilities exponential
So welcome, little one, to this beautiful world
May your life be filled with joy, love, and pearls
May you always shine bright and never dim
A new chapter has begun, let the adventure begin.

2. Childhood

Childhood is a time of magic and wonder
Where each moment is a new adventure to ponder
A world full of imagination and play
Where laughter and joy rule the day
Running through fields, climbing trees
Playing with friends, feeling the breeze
Chasing after butterflies and bees
These are the memories that childhood frees
From first steps to learning to ride a bike
From silly jokes to pillow fights
From building forts to flying kites
Childhood is a world full of delights
Days seem longer, time moves slower
With endless possibilities to discover
From finger painting to making mud pies
Every moment is a precious surprise
But childhood is fleeting, it doesn't last
It's a moment in time that goes by so fast
Soon, we'll grow up and leave it behind
But the memories and the joy will always stay in our minds
So let us cherish our childhood days
And hold onto the magic in so many ways
For it's a time of innocence and grace

A time that we can never replace.

3. Adolescence

In adolescence's stormy seas,
Where emotions run deep,
I navigated choppy waves,
And struggled hard to keep.
I questioned all that I had known,
And searched for my own truth,
I rebelled against authority,
And longed for days of youth.
I dreamed of all that lay ahead,
And yearned for independence,
But feared the choices I must make,
And consequences immense.
I loved with all my heart and soul,
And suffered heartbreak's pain,
And learned that life's a journey long,
With many twists and lanes.
Oh, adolescence, time of change,
Of growth and transformation,
When every step brings new insights,
And moments of elation.
Now older, I look back on those,
Exciting, turbulent years,
And see how they have shaped my life,

And dried my youthful tears.

4. Young Love

Young love, oh sweet and heady thing,
That makes the heart take flight,
It fills the soul with wondrous joy,
And fills the world with light.
It starts with shy and furtive glances,
And innocent, sweet smiles,
And grows into a burning passion,
That lasts for many miles.
It's like a rosebud, just unfurled,
That's bathed in morning dew,
It's like a gentle summer breeze,
That cools the skin anew.
Young love, that makes the heart beat fast,
And sets the blood afire,
It's like a symphony of sound,
That fills the soul's desire.
It's holding hands and whispered words,
And secrets shared alone,
It's sweet caresses, stolen kisses,
And hearts that beat as one.
Oh, young love, how sweet and pure,
How beautiful and true,
It's like a flame that burns so bright,

And makes the world anew.
Now older, I look back on those,
Sweet moments long gone by,
And cherish them as precious gems,
That still make my heart sigh.

5. Heartbreak

Heartbreak, oh cruel and bitter thing,
That shatters dreams apart,
It tears the soul asunder and
Leaves naught but broken heart.
It starts with tears and endless pain,
And gnaws at every thought,
It robs the world of colors bright,
And leaves us lost and fraught.
It's like a winter storm that rages,
And covers all in snow,
It's like a thunderous rain that pours,
And drowns us with its woe.
Heartbreak, that makes the heart feel heavy,
And fills the eyes with tears,
It's like a dagger through the soul,
That pierces deep and sears.
It's lonely nights and empty beds,
And silence all around,
It's memories that haunt us still,
And love that can't be found.
Oh, heartbreak, how it hurts so much,
And fills the world with pain,
It's like a wound that never heals,

And leaves a lasting stain.
Now older, I look back on those,
Dark days of pain and strife,
And see how they have made me strong,
And given me new life.

6. Marriage

Marriage, oh blessed and sacred bond,
That binds two hearts as one,
It's like a dance of two souls,
That lasts until life's done.
It starts with vows of love and faith,
And rings that seal the bond,
It's promises to cherish and
Protect until beyond.
It's shared laughter and gentle smiles,
And secrets kept between,
It's holding hands and long embraces,
And love that's evergreen.
It's building a life together,
And weathering the storms,
It's facing trials with a united front,
And never feeling torn.
Marriage, that makes the heart feel whole,
And fills the soul with light,
It's like a journey that two take,
Through darkness and through bright.
It's growing old and sharing dreams,
And memories that bind,
It's knowing that through thick and thin,

Together we will find.
Oh, marriage, how it brings such joy,
And fills the world with grace,
It's like a flower that forever blooms,
And puts a smile on the face.
Now older, I look back on those,
Sweet years with love and pride,
And cherish every moment spent,
With my beloved bride.

7. Parenthood

Parenthood, oh wondrous and blessed state,
That fills the heart with love,
It's like a journey into grace,
That leads to joys above.
It starts with tender moments shared,
And dreams of what's to be,
It's like a flower just unfurled,
That's bathed in mystery.
It's holding hands and gentle touches,
And laughter shared together,
It's like a symphony of sound,
That fills the heart with pleasure.
It's sleepless nights and endless worries,
And tears that come in waves,
It's sacrifices made with love,
And moments spent in daze.
Parenthood, that makes the heart grow strong,
And fills the soul with light,
It's like a blessing from above,
That makes everything right.
It's watching little ones grow up,
And seeing dreams take flight,
It's knowing that we made a difference,

And that everything's all right.
Oh, parenthood, how sweet and true,
How beautiful and fair,
It's like a rainbow in the sky,
That fills the world with care.
Now older, I look back on those,
Sweet years with pride and love,
And cherish every moment spent,
With my precious doves.

8. Aging

Aging, oh slow and steady march,
That creeps up with each day,
It's like a river flowing by,
That carries us away.
It starts with signs so small and slight,
And wrinkles on the skin,
It's like a breeze that softly blows,
And whispers of what's been.
It's memories of days gone by,
And stories that we've lived,
It's like a canvas painted well,
And gifts that we've been given.
It's watching loved ones grow and change,
And seeing life go by,
It's like a flower in the wind,
That slowly fades and dies.
Aging, that brings both joy and pain,
And fills the heart with tears,
It's like a bittersweet goodbye,
That echoes through the years.
It's knowing that our time is short,
And making each day count,
It's like a song that's almost done,

And echoes with its sound.
Oh, aging, how it makes us see,
The beauty of our life,
It's like a mirror that reflects,
Our struggles and our strife.
Now older, I look back on those,
Sweet moments long gone by,
And see how they have shaped my life,
And made me who am I.

9. Death

Death, the silent visitor,
Creeps into our lives, uninvited
With a cold touch, it takes us away
Leaving loved ones, heartbroken and frightened.
It comes to us all, without a warning
And leaves us wondering, what's beyond
Is there a life after death, we ask
Or is it the end, a final bond?
For some, death brings relief
From the pain and suffering of life
For others, it takes away
The ones they love, leaving them in strife.
Death is both feared and revered
A natural end to our mortal fate
It reminds us to cherish each moment
And live life without regret or hate.
Though death may seem like an end
It's also a beginning, a new start
A chance to find peace and rest
And leave behind a legacy in our heart.
So let us not fear death, my friend
For it's a part of life's grand design
Let's embrace it with grace and courage

And leave this world with love and light divine.

Nature and the World

10. Seasons

Seasons, oh cyclic and constant flow,
That marks the passing of time,
It's like a journey through nature's change,
And beauty that's so sublime.
It starts with spring's gentle embrace,
And buds that start to bloom,
It's like a promise of new life,
And hope that we resume.
It's summer's warmth and endless light,
And days that never end,
It's like a freedom that we feel,
And joy that we defend.
It's autumn's hues of red and gold,
And leaves that slowly fall,
It's like a time of sweet release,
And letting go of all.
Seasons, that bring both light and dark,
And fill the world with change,
It's like a rhythm that we know,
And patterns that arrange.
It's winter's chill and endless white,
And snow that blankets all,
It's like a time of quiet peace,

And rest that's so enthrall.
Oh, seasons, how they shape our days,
And color all we see,
It's like a story that's retold,
With beauty constantly.
Now older, I look back on those,
Sweet moments long gone by,
And cherish every season spent,
Beneath the open sky.

11. Weather

Weather, oh ever-changing force,
That shapes the world around,
It's like a dance of wind and rain,
And light that can astound.
It starts with gentle breezes blowing,
And sun that warms the earth,
It's like a promise of what's to come,
And joy that fills with mirth.
It's rain that falls in steady streams,
And nourishes the ground,
It's like a gift that nature gives,
And beauty all around.
It's snow that blankets all in white,
And covers all with peace,
It's like a dream of fairy tales,
And wonder that won't cease.
Weather, that brings both light and dark,
And fills the heart with awe,
It's like a painting in the sky,
That leaves us wanting more.
It's watching storms that rage and roar,
And lightning strikes that awe,
It's like a power that's beyond,

And leaves us filled with awe.
Oh, weather, how it shapes our days,
And colors all we see,
It's like a tapestry that's weaved,
With beauty constantly.
Now older, I look back on those,
Sweet moments long gone by,
And cherish every season spent,
Beneath the open sky.

12. Animals

Animals, oh wondrous and diverse,
That roam the earth so free,
It's like a tapestry of life,
That fills us with mystery.
It starts with creatures great and small,
And all that lies between,
It's like a symphony of sound,
That fills the world with gleam.
It's lions that roar with mighty force,
And tigers that prowl with grace,
It's like a beauty that's untamed,
And leaves us in its trace.
It's birds that soar through endless skies,
And sing with joy and cheer,
It's like a melody so sweet,
That fills our hearts with dear.
Animals, that teach us so much,
And show us how to live,
It's like a mirror to our soul,
And lessons that we give.
It's seeing the world through their eyes,
And learning from their ways,
It's like a wonderland of life,

That fills our hearts with praise.
Oh, animals, how they bring us close,
To nature's sweet embrace,
It's like a bond that lasts so long,
And fills us with such grace.
Now older, I look back on those,
Sweet moments spent in awe,
And cherish every memory made,
With creatures great and small.

13. Plants

Plants, oh humble and diverse life,
That grows upon the earth,
It's like a tapestry of green,
And beauty of great worth.
It starts with seeds that sprout with life,
And roots that dig so deep,
It's like a promise of what's to come,
And secrets that we keep.
It's flowers that bloom with fragrant scent,
And petals soft and fair,
It's like a symphony of colors,
That fills the earth with rare.
It's trees that reach up to the sky,
And branches that extend,
It's like a shelter that we seek,
And home that we defend.
Plants, that give so much to us,
And teach us how to grow,
It's like a language we must learn,
And care that we bestow.
It's watching nature's endless dance,
And rhythms that we feel,
It's like a cycle of life and death,

That's ever so surreal.
Oh, plants, how they bring us close,
To nature's sweet embrace,
It's like a bond that lasts so long,
And fills us with such grace.
Now older, I look back on those,
Sweet moments spent in awe,
And cherish every memory made,
With plants both big and small.

14. Landscapes

Landscape, oh vast and varied scene,
That stretches far and wide,
It's like a canvas painted by nature,
And beauty that can't be denied.
It starts with mountains that touch the sky,
And valleys down below,
It's like a contrast of height and depth,
And colors that constantly flow.
It's deserts that stretch out so far,
And dunes that rise and fall,
It's like a picture of endless sand,
And stories that we recall.
It's oceans that cover the earth,
And waves that crash and break,
It's like a force of power and might,
And journeys that we undertake.
Landscape, that brings us closer still,
To nature's wondrous grace,
It's like a journey through the world,
And moments we can't replace.
It's forests that stretch out for miles,
And canopy that's so grand,
It's like a world of life and green,

And mysteries we understand.
Oh, landscape, how it speaks to us,
And shows us what is true,
It's like a mirror of our world,
And beauty that's ever new.
Now older, I look back on those,
Sweet moments spent in awe,
And cherish every landscape seen,
Beneath the open sky.

15. The Sky

The sky, oh vast and endless expanse,
That stretches far and wide,
It's like a canvas painted by nature,
And beauty that can't be denied.
It starts with sunrise's gentle glow,
And colors that fill the air,
It's like a promise of what's to come,
And hope that we can share.
It's midday's bright and endless blue,
And clouds that slowly move,
It's like a freedom that we feel,
And moments that we prove.
It's sunset's hues of red and gold,
And stars that slowly emerge,
It's like a time of sweet release,
And calm that we submerge.
The sky, that brings us closer still,
To nature's wondrous grace,
It's like a journey through the world,
And moments we can't replace.
It's moon that glows so bright and clear,
And constellations we seek,
It's like a story that's retold,

And mysteries that we keep.
Oh, sky, how it speaks to us,
And shows us what is true,
It's like a mirror of our world,
And beauty that's ever new.
Now older, I look back on those,
Sweet moments spent in awe,
And cherish every sky I've seen,
Beneath the open sky above

16. The Sea

The sea, oh vast and endless blue,
That stretches far and wide,
It's like a wonder of nature's power,
And beauty that can't be denied.
It starts with waves that rise and fall,
And tides that ebb and flow,
It's like a dance of life and death,
And secrets that we know.
It's sandy shores that meet the waves,
And cliffs that tower so high,
It's like a contrast of land and sea,
And moments that pass by.
It's schools of fish that swim so fast,
And creatures that we admire,
It's like a world beneath the waves,
And life that we aspire.
The sea, that brings us closer still,
To nature's wondrous grace,
It's like a journey through the world,
And moments we can't replace.
It's ships that sail across the waves,
And ports that welcome all,
It's like a gateway to the world,

And journeys that we recall.
Oh, sea, how it speaks to us,
And shows us what is true,
It's like a mirror of our world,
And beauty that's ever new.
Now older, I look back on those,
Sweet moments spent in awe,
And cherish every memory made,
With the sea that I adore.

17. The city

The city, oh bustling and busy place,
That teems with life and sound,
It's like a world within a world,
And energy that abounds.
It starts with streets that stretch so far,
And buildings that tower high,
It's like a symbol of human might,
And progress that can't be denied.
It's people that move with such haste,
And traffic that never slows,
It's like a rhythm of city life,
And moments that come and go.
It's lights that shine so bright at night,
And neon signs that flicker,
It's like a promise of fun and thrills,
And experiences that we seek.
The city, that brings us closer still,
To human spirit and pride,
It's like a journey through the world,
And cultures that collide.
It's museums that house art and culture,
And theaters that stage plays,
It's like a celebration of creativity,

And inspiration that stays.
Oh, city, how it speaks to us,
And shows us what we can be,
It's like a mirror of our world,
And dreams that we can see.
Now older, I look back on those,
Sweet moments spent in the city,
And cherish every memory made,
With the spirit that never quits.

18. Travel

Travel, oh the thrill of the open road,
That beckons us to explore,
It's like a call to adventure,
And wonders we can't ignore.
It starts with maps and plans in hand,
And destinations we seek,
It's like a promise of what's to come,
And memories that we'll keep.
It's trains that whistle and chug along,
And planes that soar so high,
It's like a journey through the skies,
And places that we'll try.
It's roads that wind through valleys and hills,
And vistas that take our breath,
It's like a connection to the world,
And a feeling of freedom and depth.
The travel that brings us closer still,
To places we've never been,
It's like a window into the world,
And cultures that we've seen.
It's food that tantalizes our taste buds,
And music that moves our soul,
It's like a celebration of life,

And the stories that we've told.
Oh, travel, how it speaks to us,
And shows us what is true,
It's like a mirror of our world,
And the beauty that we pursue.
Now older, I look back on those,
Sweet moments spent on the road,
And cherish every memory made,
With the places that I've roamed.

Society and Humanity

19. Politics

In halls of power, the games begin
A dance of words, a fight to win
The players gather, their hands are dealt
The stakes are high, the air is felt
Ideals clash, agendas collide
Each side claims to be on the right side
The voices rise, the debates rage on
The quest for power, never gone
Behind the scenes, the deals are made
A web of influence, a price is paid
The game of politics, a power play
The people's voice, a pawn to sway
Elections come, promises abound
The people's hopes, their dreams surround
The leaders chosen, the nation's fate
In their hands, to make or break
But when the dust settles, the game goes on
The players shift, the battles won
The cycle repeats, the power game
Politics, a never-ending aim.

20. Justice

Justice, oh noble virtue fair,
Thou art a beacon bright and rare,
A guiding light for all to see,
And in thy light, all souls are free.
With even hand and impartial eye,
Thou weigh'st the scales of truth on high,
And in the balance of thy might,
The wrong is crushed, the right takes flight.
Thy sword is swift, thy voice is strong,
Thou art the defender of the wronged,
The shield for those who cannot fight,
And in thy care, all things are right.
From ancient days till present time,
Thou hast been the guard of the sublime,
The symbol of a just and fair world,
And in thy name, truth is unfurled.
So let us honor thee, oh Justice great,
And let us keep thy flame alight,
For in thy care, we shall prevail,
And in thy sight, all wrongs shall fail.

21. War

Amidst the clash of swords and shields,
The screams of battle, and bloody fields,
The ravages of war doth reign,
And all that's pure is rent in twain.
For though some may seek glory bold,
And tales of valor may be told,
The truth of war is harsh and cruel,
A deadly game, a bloody duel.
In war, the innocent suffer most,
Their homes destroyed, their lives engrossed,
Their dreams of peace are shattered, lost,
And all that's left is pain and cost.
The soldier's heart is filled with woe,
For all they love, they must forego,
Their homes, their families, their joys,
In war, they are mere battle toys.
So let us pray for peace and love,
And seek the guidance from above,
For war brings only pain and strife,
And all that's left is a shattered life.

22. Peace

Oh, peaceful world, so bright and fair,
Thou art the dream beyond compare,
The vision of a tranquil earth,
Where all is kind, and all is worth.
In thee, the heart finds rest and peace,
And all its troubles doth release,
For in thy gentle, loving embrace,
The soul finds solace and sweet grace.
No more the roar of war and strife,
No more the fear of loss and life,
For in thy arms, all hearts are one,
And all our battles are undone.
In thee, the birds sing sweetly free,
And nature blooms abundantly,
For in thy realm, all things are calm,
And all that's wild, finds gentle balm.
So let us strive for peace and love,
And seek the guidance from above,
For in thy reign, all souls are blessed,
And all that's good, is truly expressed.

23. Social issues

Amidst the bustling streets and noise,
The world is filled with social poise,
With issues that affect us all,
And make us stumble, trip and fall.
From poverty to inequality,
From racism to bigotry,
The world is plagued with wounds so deep,
That some may never truly sleep.
For every soul that's left behind,
For every voice that's lost in time,
The world is poorer for their pain,
And all their struggles, wrought in vain.
So let us rise and take a stand,
And lend a helping, guiding hand,
For in our love, and in our care,
We can help heal the wounds laid bare.
Let us seek justice and equality,
And fight for all humanity,
For in our hearts, we hold the key,
To make the world a better place to be.
For every social issue we face,
There's hope and love to take its place,
And with our strength, and with our will,

We can change the world, and make it still.

24. Religion

Oh, religion, thou art a guide,
A light that shines both far and wide,
A pathway to the divine grace,
And all the mysteries of space.
In thee, we find a moral code,
A set of rules to bear our load,
And in thy teachings, we find peace,
And all our doubts and fears release.
For every soul that seeks the truth,
And all the beauty of its youth,
Religion is a beacon bright,
A star to guide us through the night.
From Christianity to Islam,
From Buddhism to Hinduism,
The world is filled with faith and hope,
And all the ways that humans cope.
So let us seek the divine light,
And strive to do what's good and right,
For in our hearts, we hold the key,
To make religion a unity.
For every path that we may take,
There's love and kindness to partake,
And with our faith, and with our will,

We can find peace, and love, and still.

25. Philosophy

Oh, philosophy, thou art a muse,
A source of knowledge and of views,
A deep reflection on the mind,
And all the questions of mankind.
In thee, we find a quest for truth,
A search for meaning, and for proof,
And in thy wisdom, we find light,
And all the ways to live aright.
For every soul that seeks to know,
And all the mysteries that doth sow,
Philosophy is a journey grand,
A path to seek, a goal to stand.
From Plato to Aristotle,
From Descartes to Nietzsche's thistle,
The world is filled with thoughts and dreams,
And all the ways that humans scheme.
So let us ponder, and reflect,
And strive to find what we neglect,
For in our thoughts, and in our will,
We can find answers to fulfill.
For every question we may ask,
There's beauty in the thoughtful task,
And with our mind, and with our will,

We can find truth, and peace, and still.

26. Art

Oh, art, thou art a wondrous thing,
A beauty that makes our hearts sing,
A reflection of the human soul,
And all the ways we seek to grow.
In thee, we find a world of grace,
A realm where dreams can find their place,
And in thy canvas, we find truth,
And all the ways to renew youth.
For every soul that seeks to see,
And all the wonders that can be,
Art is a window to the heart,
A way to express, and to impart.
From Michelangelo's Sistine,
To Van Gogh's starry, midnight scene,
The world is filled with art and style,
And all the ways that humans smile.
So let us embrace, and create,
And strive to find what we relate,
For in our art, and in our will,
We can find beauty, and fulfill.
For every stroke we make with care,
There's wonder in the colors rare,
And with our hand, and with our will,

We can make art, and love, and still.

27. Music

Oh, music, thou art a magic spell,
A symphony that casts its spell,
A language that transcends all bounds,
And all the ways that humans sound.
In thee, we find a world of joy,
A realm where emotions can deploy,
And in thy rhythm, we find peace,
And all our worries, we release.
For every soul that seeks to hear,
And all the notes that doth appear,
Music is a gateway to the heart,
A way to feel, and to impart.
From Bach to Beethoven's ninth,
To Mozart's melodies so fine,
The world is filled with music's might,
And all the ways that humans light.
So let us dance, and sing, and play,
And let our emotions find their way,
For in our music, and in our will,
We can find beauty, and fulfill.
For every chord we play with care,
There's wonder in the notes we share,
And with our voice, and with our skill,

We can make music, and love, and still.

28. Literature

Oh, literature, thou art a realm divine,
A universe of stories that intertwine,
A sanctuary for the human mind,
And all the ways we seek to find.
In thee, we find a world of thought,
A realm where imagination is wrought,
And in thy words, we find insight,
And all the ways to shed our light.
For every soul that seeks to read,
And all the tales that doth exceed,
Literature is a window to the soul,
A way to learn, and to console.
From Shakespeare's Hamlet to Austen's Pride,
To Tolkien's tales of Middle Earth so wide,
The world is filled with literature's might,
And all the ways that humans write.
So let us read, and write, and learn,
And let our stories take their turn,
For in our literature, and in our will,
We can find wisdom, and fulfill.
For every page we write with care,
There's wonder in the words we share,
And with our pen, and with our skill,

We can make literature, and love, and still.

29. Science

Oh, science, thou art a noble quest,
A pursuit that puts our minds to the test,
A journey into the unknown,
And all the ways we seek to be shown.
In thee, we find a world of fact,
A realm where knowledge is exact,
And in thy discoveries, we find truth,
And all the ways to renew our youth.
For every soul that seeks to know,
And all the mysteries that doth sow,
Science is a key to understanding,
A way to explore, and to commanding.
From Newton's laws to Einstein's relativity,
To Darwin's theory of natural creativity,
The world is filled with science's might,
And all the ways that humans delight.
So let us study, and research, and find,
And let our curiosity take its mind,
For in our science, and in our will,
We can find progress, and fulfill.
For every experiment we conduct with care,
There's wonder in the results we share,
And with our minds, and with our skill,

We can make science, and love, and still.

30. Technology

Oh, technology, thou art a force to behold,
A power that shapes the world we behold,
An innovation that transforms our lives,
And all the ways we seek to thrive.
In thee, we find a world of possibilities,
A realm where creativity meets capabilities,
And in thy advancements, we find progress,
And all the ways to make our lives more blessed.
For every soul that seeks to invent,
And all the innovations that doth prevent,
Technology is a key to advancement,
A way to create, and to enhance.
From the printing press to the internet,
To robotics and artificial intelligence that we beget,
The world is filled with technology's might,
And all the ways that humans delight.
So let us embrace, and innovate, and explore,
And let our dreams take us to where we implore,
For in our technology, and in our will,
We can find solutions, and fulfill.
For every invention we create with care,
There's wonder in the impact we share,
And with our minds, and with our skill,

We can make technology, and love, and still.

Emotions and Perspectives

31. Happiness

Happiness is a state of being,
A feeling that sets the heart free,
It's a smile that spreads across your face,
And a warmth that fills your soul with grace.
It's the sound of laughter in the air,
And the joy that comes from being there,
It's the feeling of contentment and ease,
And the peace that comes with simple pleas.
Happiness is the sun shining bright,
And the beauty that fills our sight,
It's the sound of music that fills our ears,
And the freedom that dissolves our fears.
It's the love that we feel in our hearts,
And the connections that never fall apart,
It's the moments we cherish and hold dear,
And the memories that bring us cheer.
Happiness is the gift we give,
And the treasure that helps us live,
It's the magic that we create,
And the hope that never fades.
So let us embrace the joy of life,
And fill our hearts with happiness and light,
For it's the greatest gift we can bestow,

And the one that will forever glow.

32. Sadness

Sadness comes in like a storm,
A feeling that can't be ignored,
It's a weight that pulls us down,
And a darkness that surrounds.
It's the tears that fall from our eyes,
And the pain that we try to disguise,
It's the ache that fills our hearts,
And the sorrow that tears us apart.
Sadness is the silence that prevails,
And the emptiness that never fails,
It's the memories that haunt our minds,
And the moments we wish to rewind.
It's the absence of love and care,
And the feeling that no one is there,
It's the loneliness that we endure,
And the longing for a love so pure.
Sadness is a bitter pill to swallow,
And a burden that's hard to follow,
But it's a part of the human heart,
And a feeling that will never depart.
So let us embrace our sadness,
And allow it to fill us with its madness,
For it's a reminder of our humanity,

And a path towards our inner sanctity.

33. Anger

Anger is a fire that burns within,
A flame that can scorch and singe our skin,
It rises up and consumes us whole,
Leaving us with an emptiness that takes its toll.
Anger can be righteous, a force for good,
A passion that drives us to fight as we should,
Against injustice, cruelty, and pain,
To make the world a better place again.
But anger can also be a poison,
A toxic brew that corrodes our reason,
Blinding us to empathy and love,
And leaving us stranded, alone, and unloved.
It's easy to give in to the anger inside,
To let it take over and become our guide,
But we must resist its seductive call,
And learn to control it before we fall.
For anger can be a tool or a weapon,
A source of strength or a source of deception,
So let us use it wisely, with care,
To build a better world that we can all share.
Let us harness its power for good,
To fight for justice, to stand where we should,
And in the end, let us remember this,

That anger is a choice, not a kiss.

34. Hope

Hope is a light that shines within,
A beacon that guides us through thick and thin,
It gives us courage to face the night,
And fills our hearts with a warm, gentle light.
Hope is a dream that we hold dear,
A vision of a future that's bright and clear,
It inspires us to reach for the stars,
And reminds us that there's no limit to who we are.
With hope, we can weather any storm,
And face any challenge with a spirit that's warm,
For hope is the fuel that drives us on,
And gives us the strength to carry on.
In times of darkness, hope is a flame,
That burns bright and steady, with no shame,
It shows us that there's always a way,
And that even the darkest night turns to day.
So hold onto hope, and never let go,
For it's the seed that can help us grow,
And when we nurture it with love and care,
It blooms into a future that's bright and fair.
Hope is the promise of a new dawn,
The assurance that we can all carry on,
And though life may be tough, and trials may come,

With hope in our hearts, we'll never be undone.

35. Despair

Despair is a weight that drags us down,
A darkness that seems to surround,
It suffocates and steals our breath,
Leaving us feeling alone in death.
Despair is a pit that we fall into,
A bottomless chasm of pain and rue,
It makes us feel like we're all alone,
And that nothing we do can make it home.
In times of despair, hope seems far away,
And the light of day turns to shades of grey,
It's hard to see a future that's bright,
When we're caught in the grip of such a fright.
But even in the depths of despair,
There's a glimmer of light that's always there,
A spark of hope that we can hold,
And use to break free from the grip so cold.
It's easy to feel lost in the dark,
To forget that there's a path to embark,
But with time and love, we can rise above,
And find the strength to spread our wings and fly like a dove.
Despair may be a heavy load,
But we can carry it along the road,
And even when the journey's tough,

We can find the way, and we'll make it through, and that's enough.
So hold onto the hope within,
And let it guide you through thick and thin,
For even in the darkest hour,
There's always a way to find the power.

36. Fear

Fear is a force that can paralyze,
A weight that can make us compromise,
It's the voice that whispers in our ear,
Telling us to cower and stay clear.
Fear can be a warning that we heed,
A signal to watch out and take heed,
But it can also hold us back,
Making us afraid to make the right attack.
In times of fear, we can lose our way,
And forget the strength that we hold each day,
But if we can stand tall and face our fright,
We'll find the power to stand and fight.
Fear may be a foe that we must face,
But it's also an opportunity to embrace,
To grow and learn and find our might,
And to conquer the darkness and see the light.
With courage, we can break free from the chains,
That hold us back and cause us pains,
And rise above the fear that we once knew,
To find the strength to follow through.
So when fear comes knocking at our door,
Let's take a stand and show it the door,
For we are stronger than we may believe,

And with each step, we can achieve.

37. Courage

Courage is a flame that burns within,
A light that guides us through thick and thin,
It's the strength that we find when we're afraid,
And the hope that we hold when we're dismayed.
Courage is a voice that whispers in our ear,
Telling us to rise and conquer our fear,
It's the spark that ignites the fire within,
And the force that drives us to never give in.
With courage, we can face any foe,
And overcome any obstacle that we may know,
For when we hold onto our inner might,
We can rise above any challenge, and we'll shine so bright.
In times of darkness, courage is the light,
That guides us through the depths of the night,
It's the hope that we cling to in despair,
And the love that we find when nothing seems fair.
So hold onto courage, and let it guide you,
Through the struggles and the battles that we all go through,
For with each step, and with each breath,
We can face any challenge and conquer it with grace.
Courage is the heart that beats within,
The soul that pushes us to begin,
And with each moment, and with each step,

We can rise above, and we'll never forget.

38. Gratitude

Gratitude is a gift that we can give,
A way of life that helps us truly live,
It's the light that shines in the darkest hour,
And the power that gives us strength and power.
Gratitude is the art of saying thanks,
For all the blessings that we have in our ranks,
For the people who love us and the joy they bring,
And for the beauty of life that we get to sing.
With gratitude, we can find the light,
That makes even the darkest day so bright,
For when we focus on the good that we see,
We open up our hearts and let the love be.
In times of sadness, gratitude can heal,
And help us find the strength to truly feel,
The love and beauty that's all around,
And the joy that we can share and abound.
So let's hold onto gratitude, each and every day,
And let it be the light that guides our way,
For when we're grateful for all that we have,
We'll find the love and joy that truly make us glad.
Gratitude is the heart that beats within,
The soul that helps us truly begin,
And with each breath, and with each step,

We can find the love, and we'll never forget.

39. Regret

Regret is a weight that we carry within,
A burden that reminds us of where we've been,
It's the voice that whispers in our ear,
Telling us that we've made mistakes, and filled with fear.
Regret can be a lesson that we learn,
A chance to grow and for our soul to yearn,
But it can also hold us back,
Making us feel like we're under attack.
In times of regret, we can feel alone,
And wonder if we'll ever find our way home,
But if we can find the courage to face our past,
We can make amends and find peace that'll forever last.
Regret may be a foe that we must face,
But it's also an opportunity to embrace,
To grow and learn and make amends,
And to find the strength to make new friends.
With honesty, we can break free from the chains,
That hold us back and cause us pains,
And rise above the regret that we once knew,
To find the strength to follow through.
So when regret comes knocking at our door,
Let's take a stand and show it the door,
For we are stronger than we may believe,

And with each step, we can achieve.

40. Reflection

Reflection is a mirror to the soul,
A way to see ourselves, to be whole,
It's the light that shines on our deepest fears,
And the power that helps us to persevere.
Reflection is the art of looking within,
To see the truth of where we've been,
For when we take the time to truly reflect,
We can see the beauty and the imperfections that we project.
With reflection, we can find the peace we seek,
And the answers to the questions that we keep,
For when we sit in silence and truly listen,
We can hear the voice that'll guide us to the right decision.
In times of chaos, reflection can calm the mind,
And help us leave the negative thoughts behind,
For when we take the time to look inside,
We can find the peace that we need to abide.
So let's hold onto reflection, each and every day,
And let it be the light that guides our way,
For when we take the time to truly reflect,
We can find the beauty and the peace that we so desperately expect.
Reflection is the heart that beats within,
The soul that helps us truly begin,

And with each breath, and with each step,
We can find the love, and we'll never forget.

Personal Experiences

41. Dreams

Dreams are the seeds of our imagination,
The spark that ignites our inspiration,
They're the gateway to what we can achieve,
And the hope that we can truly believe.
Dreams are the world that we create,
A vision of our future, that we contemplate,
They're the fuel that drives us to be more,
And the spirit that helps us to soar.
With dreams, we can reach for the sky,
And find the courage to never say die,
For when we hold onto our inner might,
We can rise above any challenge, and we'll shine so bright.
In times of darkness, dreams are the light,
That guides us through the depths of the night,
It's the hope that we cling to in despair,
And the love that we find when nothing seems fair.
So let's hold onto our dreams, and never let go,
For they're the source of our strength, and the reason we grow,
For with each step, and with each breath,
We can make our dreams a reality, and live with no regret.
Dreams are the heart that beats within,
The soul that pushes us to begin,
And with each moment, and with each step,

We can achieve anything, and we'll never forget.

42. Memories

Memories are the treasures we hold,
The stories of our lives, so bold,
They're the reminders of where we've been,
And the love and joy that we've seen.
Memories are the colors of our past,
A canvas of moments that forever last,
They're the emotions that we can't forget,
And the lessons that we'll never regret.
With memories, we can travel back in time,
To relive the moments that were once so fine,
For when we hold onto the memories we've made,
We can find the strength to never be afraid.
In times of sorrow, memories can heal,
And bring us comfort, and the love we feel,
It's the light that shines through the darkest hour,
And the power that gives us strength and power.
So let's hold onto memories, and cherish each one,
For they're the pieces of us that can never be undone,
For with each breath, and with each step,
We can remember the love, and we'll never forget.
Memories are the heart that beats within,
The soul that helps us truly begin,
And with each moment, and with each step,

We can cherish the memories, and we'll never forget.

43. Friendship

Friendship is a bond that we hold so dear,
A connection that brings us hope and cheer,
It's the laughter that fills our hearts with joy,
And the love that we find in each other's joy.
Friendship is the light that guides us through,
The tough times that we all go through,
It's the shoulder we lean on when we're in need,
And the words of encouragement that help us to succeed.
With friendship, we can conquer any fear,
And know that someone will always be near,
For when we hold onto the bonds we've made,
We can find the strength to never be afraid.
In times of chaos, friendship can bring calm,
And help us to find the strength to carry on,
It's the gift that we give and receive in turn,
And the love that we find when we're in need of concern.
So let's hold onto our friendships, each and every day,
And let them be the light that guides our way,
For with each step, and with each breath,
We can cherish the love, and we'll never forget.
Friendship is the heart that beats within,
The soul that helps us truly begin,
And with each moment, and with each step,

We can hold onto our friendships, and we'll never forget.

44. Loneliness

Loneliness is a weight that we all bear,
A feeling that we sometimes cannot bear,
It's the ache that we feel in our hearts,
And the emptiness that tears us apart.
Loneliness is the silence that fills our days,
The absence of laughter in so many ways,
It's the longing for a connection that's gone,
And the fear that we'll be forever alone.
With loneliness, we can feel so lost,
And wonder if we'll ever pay the cost,
For when we're alone, it's hard to find hope,
And the light that we need to help us to cope.
In times of darkness, loneliness can be,
The pain that we try so hard to set free,
It's the reminder of what we used to have,
And the longing for the love that we can't grab.
So let's hold onto hope, and never let go,
For with hope, the seeds of love can grow,
For with each step, and with each breath,
We can find the connection, and we'll never forget.
Loneliness is the heart that beats within,
The soul that helps us truly begin,
And with each moment, and with each step,

We can break the chains of loneliness, and we'll never forget.

45. Self-discovery

Self-discovery is a journey we all take,
A path we walk, and choices we make,
It's the exploration of who we are,
And the journey to find our own shining star.
Self-discovery is the key that unlocks the door,
To the potential that we all hold and more,
It's the realization of our strengths and weaknesses,
And the courage to confront our fears and meekness.
With self-discovery, we can find our true self,
And unlock the power that's within ourselves,
For when we embrace who we truly are,
We can find the confidence to raise the bar.
In times of doubt, self-discovery can bring clarity,
And help us find our true identity,
It's the journey that we all must take,
To find our place in this world, and our own unique stake.
So let's embrace the journey, each and every day,
And let self-discovery lead the way,
For with each step, and with each breath,
We can find the courage, and we'll never forget.
Self-discovery is the heart that beats within,
The soul that helps us truly begin,
And with each moment, and with each step,

We can find the truth, and we'll never forget.

46. Ambition

Ambition is a fire that burns so bright,
A passion that fuels us, both day and night,
It's the drive that pushes us to achieve,
And the courage to chase the dreams we believe.
Ambition is the vision that guides our way,
The force that helps us seize the day,
It's the strength that helps us face the fear,
And the power that helps us persevere.
With ambition, we can reach new heights,
And conquer any challenge that comes in sight,
For when we aim high and never give up,
We can find the success that we truly want.
In times of struggle, ambition can bring hope,
And help us find the strength to cope,
It's the spark that ignites our soul,
And the inspiration that helps us stay whole.
So let's embrace our ambition, each and every day,
And let it be the light that guides our way,
For with each step, and with each breath,
We can achieve our dreams, and we'll never forget.
Ambition is the heart that beats within,
The soul that helps us truly begin,
And with each moment, and with each step,

We can chase our dreams, and we'll never forget.

47. Success

Success is a journey we all take,
A path we walk, and choices we make,
It's the realization of our goals and dreams,
And the courage to swim against the streams.
Success is the fruit of our hard work and dedication,
The result of our efforts and determination,
It's the feeling of pride and accomplishment,
And the sense of fulfillment that leaves us content.
With success, we can reach new heights,
And make the impossible come to life,
For when we set our goals and stay focused,
We can achieve anything that's within our locus.
In times of doubt, success can bring clarity,
And help us find our true identity,
It's the reminder of what we're capable of,
And the inspiration to continue our journey of love.
So let's celebrate our success, each and every day,
And let it be the force that guides our way,
For with each step, and with each breath,
We can make our dreams come true, and we'll never forget.
Success is the heart that beats within,
The soul that helps us truly begin,
And with each moment, and with each step,

We can reach for the stars, and we'll never forget.

48. Failure

Failure is a part of life we all must face,
A challenge that we all must embrace,
It's the lesson that teaches us to grow,
And the path that leads us to the seeds we sow.
Failure is the stepping stone to success,
The bridge that helps us to progress,
It's the reminder that we're not perfect,
And the inspiration to never quit.
With failure, we can learn from our mistakes,
And try again with each step that it takes,
For when we face adversity with resilience,
We can find the courage to rise with brilliance.
In times of struggle, failure can bring hope,
And help us find new ways to cope,
It's the teacher that shows us the way,
And the motivation to seize the day.
So let's embrace our failures, each and every one,
And let them be the building blocks of what we've become,
For with each step, and with each breath,
We can rise again, and we'll never forget.
Failure is the heart that beats within,
The soul that helps us truly begin,
And with each moment, and with each step,

We can find success, and we'll never forget.

49. Inspiration

Inspiration is the spark that lights the fire,
The force that helps us aim higher,
It's the muse that leads us to create,
And the energy that fuels our fate.
Inspiration is the wind beneath our wings,
The voice that whispers of greater things,
It's the courage to chase our dreams,
And the strength to overcome life's extremes.
With inspiration, we can see the world anew,
And find the beauty in all that we do,
For when we're inspired, we're unstoppable,
And our dreams become more than just possible.
In times of darkness, inspiration can bring light,
And help us find the strength to fight,
It's the hope that lifts us when we're down,
And the drive that helps us wear the crown.
So let's seek out inspiration, each and every day,
And let it guide us along the way,
For with each step, and with each breath,
We can find our purpose, and we'll never forget.
Inspiration is the heart that beats within,
The soul that helps us truly begin,
And with each moment, and with each step,

We can change the world, and we'll never forget.

50. Creativity

Creativity is the power to imagine,
The ability to see what's hidden,
It's the spark that ignites our soul,
And the force that helps us make things whole.
Creativity is the gift that we all possess,
The magic that we use to express,
It's the way we bring our dreams to life,
And the path that leads us to new heights.
With creativity, we can paint our world,
And create something from nothing, unfurled,
For when we let our imagination roam,
Our possibilities turn into an endless home.
In times of stagnation, creativity can bring change,
And help us see beyond the norm's range,
It's the push that inspires us to evolve,
And the drive that helps us reach new resolve.
So let's embrace our creativity, each and every day,
And let it take us on a wild ride, come what may,
For with each step, and with each breath,
We can make magic, and we'll never forget.
Creativity is the heart that beats within,
The soul that helps us truly begin,
And with each moment, and with each step,

We can make art, and we'll never forget.

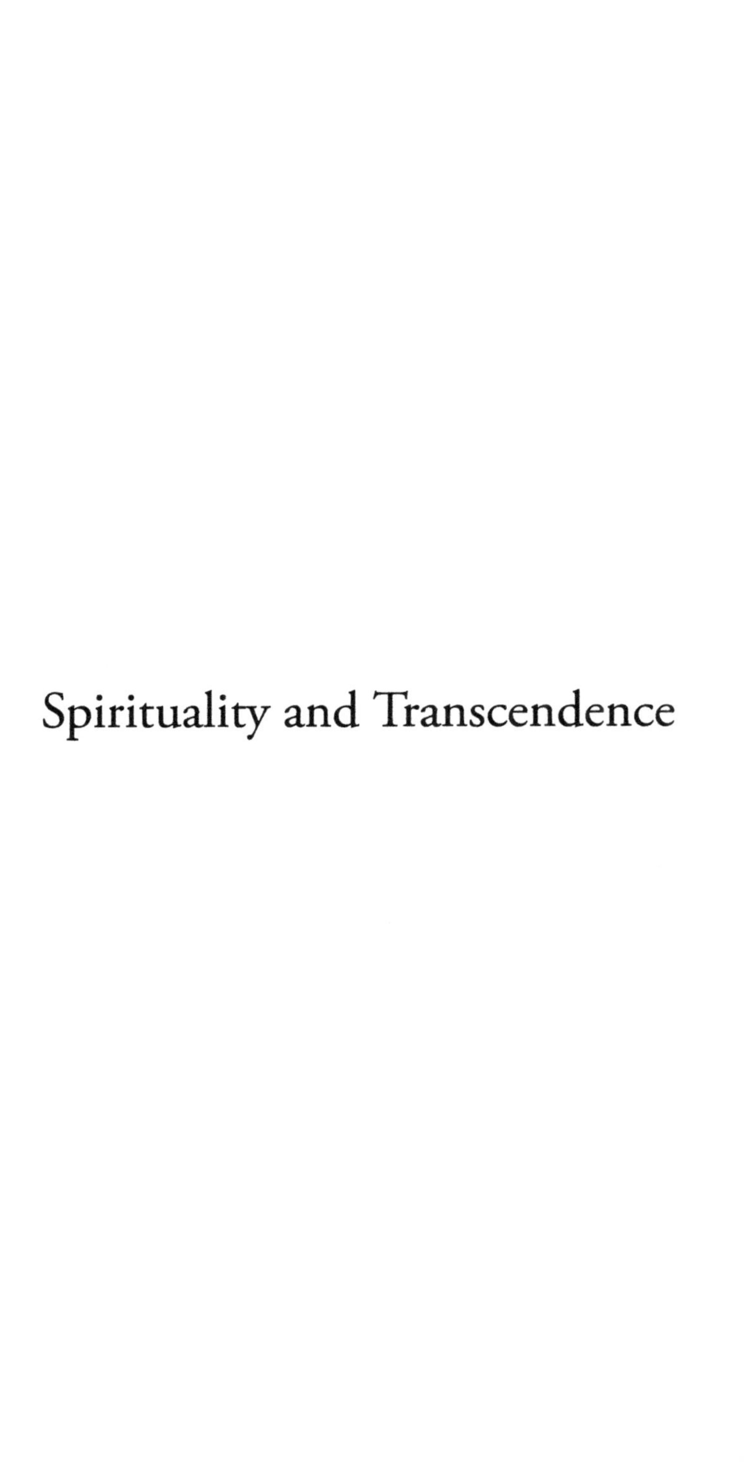

Spirituality and Transcendence

51. Faith

Faith is the light that guides us on our way,
The unwavering trust that keeps fears at bay,
It's the assurance that we are not alone,
And the strength to face the unknown.
Faith is the foundation of our hope,
The anchor that helps us to cope,
It's the belief that all will be well,
And the source of our inner peace that we can tell.
With faith, we can weather life's storms,
And find the strength to carry on,
For when we hold onto our beliefs,
Our spirits soar and our doubts fall like leaves.
In times of darkness, faith can bring light,
And help us see beyond the night,
It's the hand that lifts us up when we fall,
And the voice that whispers "you can do it all."
So let's hold onto our faith, each and every day,
And trust that it will lead us on the way,
For with each step, and with each breath,
We can find our purpose, and we'll never forget.
Faith is the heart that beats within,
The soul that helps us truly begin,
And with each moment, and with each step,

We can find our way, and we'll never forget.

52. Doubt

Doubt is the shadow that follows us around,
The whisper that fills our mind with sound,
It's the fear that we might be wrong,
And the uncertainty that we can't be strong.
Doubt is the thief that steals our confidence,
The barrier that blocks our resilience,
It's the voice that tells us we can't,
And the force that makes our dreams seem scant.
With doubt, we can lose our way,
And let our fears lead us astray,
For when we give in to our uncertainties,
Our opportunities turn into disabilities.
In times of confusion, doubt can take hold,
And leave us feeling helpless and cold,
It's the voice that tells us to stay back,
And the force that makes us feel out of whack.
So let's face our doubts, each and every day,
And find the strength to push them away,
For with each step, and with each breath,
We can find our power, and we'll never forget.
Doubt is the challenge that tests our will,
The obstacle that we can overcome still,
And with each moment, and with each step,

We can find our truth, and we'll never forget.

53. Mysticism

In the depths of the night, when all is still,
And the stars in the sky twinkle with a thrill,
There lies a realm beyond our sight,
A place of magic, of wonder and light.
It's the world of mysticism, the realm of the divine,
Where the veil between our world and beyond is fine,
It's the place where spirits roam free,
And the soul finds its ultimate key.
In the silence of the mind, when all is calm,
And the heart is open like a balm,
There lies a journey to the unknown,
A quest for the essence, a path to be shown.
It's the journey of mysticism, the way of the seeker,
Where the truth is unveiled, and the wisdom is deeper,
It's the way to connect to the universal whole,
And the source of the spiritual soul.
In the whispers of the wind, when all is hushed,
And the trees in the forest sway, unconcerned and lush,
There lies a call to something greater,
A yearning for the mystical, a quest for the creator.
It's the call of mysticism, the longing for the divine,
Where the heart finds its home, and the spirit can shine,
It's the way to transcend our earthly binds,

And find the sacred within our minds.
So let us journey into the world of mysticism,
With open hearts, and a spirit of optimism,
For in this realm of magic and wonder,
We can find our purpose, and our souls can thunder.

54. Enlightenment

Enlightenment, a journey divine,
Where the soul transcends the confines of time,
A path to freedom, a quest for truth,
Where the mind expands, and the heart finds its root.
It's a journey of the self, a quest for the soul,
Where the illusions of the world lose their hold,
And the light of consciousness shines within,
Revealing the essence of all that's been.
With each step, the veils are lifted,
And the mysteries of life are slowly gifted,
The mind expands, the heart opens wide,
And the essence of the universe is found inside.
Enlightenment, the ultimate goal,
Where the ego dissolves, and the spirit is whole,
A state of being, where love abounds,
And the soul finds peace, in its own profound.
It's a journey of the brave, a quest for the wise,
Where the heart is the compass, and the mind the guide,
And the light of truth, forever shines,
Guiding the way, through the ups and downs of time.
So let us journey on, to the world of enlightenment,
With open hearts, and a spirit of wonderment,
For in this realm of truth and light,

Our souls can find their ultimate flight.

55. Nature of reality

The nature of reality, a mystery profound,
A puzzle unsolved, a truth yet to be found,
It's the fabric of existence, the essence of being,
A realm of wonder, beyond our way of seeing.
It's a world of duality, of light and dark,
Of pleasure and pain, and of truth and mark,
It's a place of wonder, where the unknown resides,
And the mysteries of life, forever abides.
The nature of reality, a canvas so vast,
Where the laws of nature, forever contrast,
It's a world of paradox, of shadow and light,
Where the opposites unite, and the balance is right.
It's a world of perception, of subjective truth,
Where the mind creates, and the heart finds proof,
It's a world of illusion, of Maya and mirage,
Where the ego dances, and the soul finds its voyage.
The nature of reality, a mystery to explore,
A journey of wonder, of magic and more,
It's a place of potential, of infinite possibility,
Where the mind expands, and the spirit finds liberty.
So let us journey on, to the world of reality,
With open hearts, and a spirit of curiosity,
For in this realm of wonder and awe,

Our souls can find their ultimate core.

56. Purpose

In the depth of our souls, a calling awaits,
A purpose divine, that forever dictates,
It's a quest for the heart, a journey of the soul,
A calling to serve, a destiny to unfold.
For each of us, a unique path lies ahead,
A calling within, that cannot be misread,
It's a journey of passion, of courage and might,
A calling divine, that forever ignites.
Some seek to heal, with compassion and care,
To ease the suffering, of those in despair,
Some seek to create, with art and with skill,
To inspire the world, and to bend it to their will.
Some seek to teach, with knowledge and light,
To guide the way, and to make the wrong right,
Some seek to lead, with vision and grace,
To inspire the masses, and to lead the race.
And yet, no matter the path we may choose,
Or the purpose we seek, with all our muse,
We all share a common thread, a destiny to fulfill,
To make this world a better place, with love and goodwill.
So let us journey on, to the world of purpose,
With open hearts, and a spirit of service,
For in this realm of wonder and awe,

Our souls can find their ultimate law.

57. Meaning of Life

What is the meaning of this life we lead,
A question as old as time, one that we all must heed,
Is it to gather riches, to seek fame and glory,
Or is there something deeper, something more worthy?
Perhaps the answer lies not in what we gain,
But in what we give, in how we ease the pain,
Of those around us, who struggle and toil,
Who seek a better life, in this mortal coil.
For life is but a fleeting moment, a passing breath,
A chance to leave our mark, before our final rest,
To live with purpose, with passion and with love,
To make this world a better place, with every act and thought.
For in the end, it's not what we accumulate,
But the lives we touch, the love we create,
That gives our existence, a meaning and a worth,
A legacy that lives on, long after we depart from this earth.
So let us cherish each day, with gratitude and care,
And seek to live a life, that's meaningful and rare,
For in this quest for purpose, for love and for grace,
We can find the true meaning, of this life we embrace.

58. Mortality

Oh fleeting mortal, born to die,
A brief flicker of light, before the eternal night,
In this realm of time, we journey on,
Toward an inevitable fate, to which we must belong.
We walk the path of life, with a measured pace,
With each step forward, we leave behind a trace,
Of memories and moments, that we hold dear,
A legacy of love, that can withstand the fear.
For death may come, like a thief in the night,
A sudden end to all that's bright,
But what we leave behind, can never be erased,
A testament to our souls, that forever will be graced.
So let us not fear, the final hour,
For death is but a gate, to a higher power,
And in this passing, we can find a new beginning,
A release from the bonds of this mortal living.
And as we journey on, toward the great unknown,
Let us live each day, with love and kindness shown,
For in the end, it's not the length of our days,
But the depth of our love, that will forever stay.

59. Beyond the physical

Beyond the physical, lies a world unseen,
A realm of mystery, of wonder and of dream,
Where spirits roam free, and angels sing,
And the echoes of eternity, forever ring.
In this unseen world, there are no bounds,
No limits to the wonders that surround,
For here, the mind can soar and fly,
And the soul can touch the very sky.
Beyond the physical, is a world of light,
Where darkness fades, and all is right,
And the struggles of life, are left behind,
As we journey toward a greater kind.
Here, the past and future are one,
And all that's lost can be undone,
As the veil of illusion falls away,
And the true nature of being comes to play.
Beyond the physical, is a world of love,
A place of grace and blessings from above,
Where every heart can find its home,
And all can find a place to roam.
So let us not be bound by earthly chains,
But reach beyond, and embrace the eternal plane,
For in this realm of spirit and light,

We can find a world beyond our sight.

60. Epiphany

In moments of clarity, the veil is lifted,
And what once was hidden, is now gifted,
A sudden understanding, an epiphany,
That reveals the truth of our reality.
In a flash of inspiration, the mind is opened,
And the mysteries of life become awoken,
The answers we've sought, now crystal clear,
And all that once was cloudy, now disappears.
The world around us takes on new meaning,
And we see with fresh eyes, the beauty gleaming,
The path we've walked, suddenly revealed,
And the destiny that awaits, now unsealed.
With this epiphany, comes a sense of purpose,
A calling that's been waiting to surface,
And the confidence to pursue our dreams,
And step into the light, no matter how it beams.
So let us welcome these moments of insight,
Embrace them fully, with all our might,
For in these moments of epiphany,
We can discover a life of greater harmony.

9 798890 024770

Printed by Libri Plureos GmbH in Hamburg,
Germany